Yu-Gi-Oh!
S C R A P B O O K

D1529797

This is an unofficial and unauthorized project. No persons associated with Yu-Gi-Oh have given their permission to publish this book or are in any way connected with it. Although the publishers believe the contents of this book to be true at the time of publication, they do not accept any responsibility in this regard.

Modern Publishing
A Division of Unisystems, Inc.
New York, New York 10022
Printed in the U.S.A
Series UPC# 65015

THE STORY OF YU-GI-OH

Yu-Gi-Oh is the story of a high school freshman named Yugi, and his best friends, Joey, Tristan, and Téa. According to legend, five thousand years ago, ancient Egyptian pharaohs used to play a magical game (called the Shadow Game) that was very similar to Duel Monsters and involved magical ceremonies used to foresee the future and, ultimately, decide a player's destiny. The game that the pharaohs played, however, used real monsters!

With all of those magical spells and ferocious monsters unleashed on the earth, it wasn't long before things got out of hand and threatened to destroy the entire world! Luckily, a brave pharaoh came forward and prevented a catastrophe by using seven powerful magical totems.

Now, in our day, the ancient Egyptian Shadow Game has been revived in the form of a playing card

Kazuki Takahashi, the creator of YU-GI-OH, was born in 1961 in Tokyo. He started drawing comics in his teens, and made his public debut in Japan's best-selling weekly comic magazine, *Shonen Jump*, in 1991. He began drawing the comics series YU-GI-OH in 1996. The animated version of YU-GI-OH debuted in 2000 and became an immediate hit in Japan, spawning a mania that included video games, animation, and a card game, all of which boasted record sales. To date, 23 million comics have been sold and YU-GI-OH's appeal has spread across every facet of the media. Kazuki Takahashi is now known as one of Japan's foremost comic artists.

YU-GI-OH made its stunning debut in 1996 in Japan. To date, it has sold over 23 million comic books (over 33 million when including non-comic book related YU-GI-OH titles), 7.5 million video games and a staggering 3.5 billion cards.

game called Duel Monsters. Yugi's grandfather, who manages a gaming shop, introduces Yugi to the Duel Monsters game, which pits different mystical creatures against one another in wild, magical duels on a shifting battlefield filled with traps and magical pitfalls. The game, packed with awesome monsters and mighty spell-cards, becomes an obsession for Yugi and his friends. But there's more to it than meets the eye because, meanwhile, Yugi's grandfather gives Yugi an ancient Egyptian puzzle that apparently no one can solve. When Yugi unlocks the secret of the Egyptian Millennium Puzzle, he releases the powerful spirit of an Egyptian king, Yami Yugi. Because he solved the Millennium Puzzle, Yugi is rewarded with the spirit of the all-powerful game king (who becomes his alter-ego). Infused with these ancient magical energies, Yugi must now protect the world from the return of the destructive Shadow Game using cards containing legendary monsters and magical spells. Thus, Yugi sets off on a path to become the King of Duelists!

Soon after, the mysterious creator of the Duel Monsters card game, Maximillion Pegasus, kidnaps Yugi's grandfather and Yugi is drawn into a Duel Monsters competition that Pegasus has arranged. Now Yugi must duel his way through a tournament and defeat Pegasus in order to save his grandfather's soul. How will Yugi do it? Will the help of his friends, his belief in the heart of the cards, and the mysterious power of his magical Millennium Puzzle be enough? Only time will tell.

THE CHARACTERS

There are many interesting characters that inhabit the Yu-Gi-Oh universe. Here are the main characters and the major decks that they control.

YUGI MUTOU

Yugi Mutou is the main character of Yu-Gi-Oh. Yugi loves to play and solve games and lives with his grandfather, who manages a gaming shop. When Yugi was growing up, his grandfather gave him an ancient Egyptian artifact called the Millennium Puzzle to try and solve, telling him that legend had it that whoever managed to solve the puzzle would be granted dark and mysterious powers. After Yugi unlocked the puzzle's secret, something amazing happened that changed his life forever—he discovered a personality hidden deep within the puzzle that comes out whenever Yugi needs to play a game. The age-old powers of the puzzle flood out and Yugi becomes Yami Yugi, a powerful spirit who duels with many rivals. Sometimes, Yugi is forced to play by his opponent's rules, and usually beats them at their own game. While Yugi, himself, does not know the full extent of the Millennium Puzzle's power, he slowly begins to discover its mysterious links to ancient Egypt.

While his fellow freshmen at Domino High School see him only as the shy type, Yugi's best friends, Joey, Tristan, and Téa know about his secret talent. When the soul of Yugi's grandfather is stolen by the creator of the Duel Monsters card game, Pegasus J. Crawford, Yugi goes to the Duelist Kingdom to try to retrieve it.

Yugi's Deck: Black Magician Deck, with cards that support it (and some other tricks).

YAMI YUGI

The alter-ego of Yugi. Using the Millennium Puzzle, Yugi is filled with magical energy, which makes him more powerful and a master dueler. When the Millennium Puzzle activates, Yugi is filled with its magical energies and becomes Yami Yugi, his much more powerful alter ego. Not only is Yami Yugi a master dueler, but he's full of confidence and courage (unlike the usually shy Yugi).

MAXIMILLION PEGASUS

(Japanese Name: Pegasus J. Crawford)

Head of the Industrial Illusion Company, Maximillion Pegasus is the sophisticated, cultured and ingenious creator of the Duel Monsters card game which he modeled after a mysterious Egyptian game thousands of years old. While a seemingly perfect gentleman on the outside, Pegasus has many dark secrets that make him very dangerous indeed. Chief among them is the fact that his left eye has been replaced with an ancient Egyptian artifact called the Millennium Eye, a totem that gives Pegasus strange and magical powers, including the ability to read an opponent's mind. Because of this, he has never been defeated in battle. But he is equally dangerous because he is willing to do virtually anything to gain control of the Kaiba Corporation. Why? That is another of his secrets that is not revealed for quite some time.

Maximillion's Deck:
A strange combination of comedy and grossness, this Deck is built around the Toon World card (which effectively makes Toons invincible to attack, and allows attacks on an opponent directly). Additionally, the Deck has the Sacrifice and Thousand Eyes Sacrifice card, which can absorb an opponent's Monsters.

JOEY WHEELER

(Japanese Name: Katsuya Jounouchi)

Often called Jounouchi, Joey is both Yugi's best friend and his rival. Early on in the comic series, both he and another friend, Honda, pick on Yugi because he is short. When Yugi comes to their defense when they are being beat up by a larger bully, however, both become Yugi's friends, and now are almost always seen with him. Formerly a tough street kid, Joey comes to learn the value of his loyal friendship with Yugi. Although Joey's harsh background sometimes leads to hot-headed actions before he thinks things through, he has a good heart and will do anything for his friends or his younger sister, Serenity. In fact, when Yugi goes to the Duelist Kingdom to try to retrieve his grandfather's soul, Jounouchi goes with him—

but for a different reason. He needs to win the Duelist Kingdom tournament to win enough prize money to pay for an operation to fix his sister's failing eyesight.

> **Joey's Deck:**
> A Warrior and Animal Warrior Deck, with a few chance cards (like the Time Magician).

Serenity Wheeler

(Japanese Name: Shizuka Jounouchi)

Joey Wheeler cares a lot about his younger sister, Serenity, who has a birth defect that is gradually causing her to go blind. Only an expensive operation (that they can only afford if Joey gets the prize money awarded for winning the Duelist Kingdom tournament) can save her from going blind. Joey and Serenity's parents divorced when they were

younger, and she was taken to another city where she lives apart from Joey.

TÉA GARDNER

(Japanese Name: Anzu Mazaki)

The only female member of the group, Téa Gardner is the voice of reason among all of Yugi's friends. A friend of Yugi's since childhood, Téa is the biggest optimist in the group, constantly encouraging everyone to believe in themselves and to never give up. While she does not play a huge role all of the time, Téa always seems to come through when she has to. In the animated series, Téa loves her friends and is willing to help them in any way she possibly can.

TRISTAN TAYLOR

(Japanese Name: Hiroto Honda)

Joey Wheeler's partner in crime, and a member of the group, Tristan comes with Yugi and Joey to the Duelist Kingdom basically for moral support. While he has some Duel Monsters cards, he doesn't play the game. Even though Joey and Tristan sometimes bicker with each other, they always protect each other when the going gets rough. Sometimes Tristan is quick to panic, but in the end he is willing to do whatever it takes to support and help his friends.

After losing a duel to Yugi, however, Kaiba makes it his ultimate goal in life to finally defeat Yugi, using whatever means necessary. He simply can't live with the fact that Yugi beat him. Although he resents Yugi, Kaiba seems to be slowly developing a degree of respect for him.

Kaiba has a younger brother named Mokuba, who shares Kaiba's passion for gaming. When Kaiba and Mokuba were being raised in an orphanage, Kaiba promised Mokuba that he would take care of him no matter what. When he finds out that Pegasus has taken his little brother, Kaiba immediately goes to the Duelist Kingdom to get him back.

MAI VALENTINE

(Japanese Name: Mai Kujaku)

Mai Valentine is a female duelist who has come to the Duelist Kindgom to win big money and test her skills. She's one of the world's top duelists and is as dangerous as she is pretty. Mai is completely self-absorbed, and is definitely not above using her charm to her advantage. Her card deck is based upon the Harpy Lady card and she uses a special card trick to get the better of her opponents. Although she is superficial to the max, there may be some hope for her if only she can learn from Yugi.

Mai's Deck:
In the Duelist Kingdom, Mai constructed a Deck focusing on the Harpy Lady, using her other cards to support it. In Battle City, she used the New Amazoness Deck, which used Amazoness cards (and also included her Harpy Ladies).

SETO KAIBA

Seto Kaiba is a high-school age student, yet he is already the president of the multi-national high-tech corporation Kaiba Corporation, and is already very

rich. His real passion, however, is the world of Duel Monsters. There, he uses his ruthless business drive to overcome any who challenge him. Kaiba has become one of the best Duel Monsters players in the world.

Seto's Deck:
A blitzkrieg-type Deck, with strong Monsters like Blue Eyes, The God of Obelisk, and Blood Vors. He also has some anti-Monster cards, such as the Deck Destruction Virus of Death.

Japanese National Duel Monsters champion. On the ship to the Duelist Kingdom, he tosses Yugi's prized Exodia cards overboard. Weevil ultimately becomes Yugi's first opponent in the Duelist Kingdom.

Weevil's Deck:

Weevil's Deck is a pure Insect-Combo Deck, composed of Insect Monsters. Since Insects are rather weak, Weevil relies on additional tricks to make the Deck effective. In the Duelist Kingdom, he used the Great Moth as his finisher. In Battle City, his finisher was the Insect Queen, with his Insect Barrier combo.

ガズィデ
Rex Raptor

(Japanese Name: Dinosaur Ryuzaki)

Rex Raptor is the Japanese National runner-up. He is vain, but not as bad as Weevil, though they often hang out together.

Rex's Deck:

Rex Raptor's Deck is composed of powerful Dinosaur Monsters; it is pure blitzkrieg. This is an easy Deck to use—big Monsters and lots of power.

MOKUBA KAIBA

Mokuba Kaiba is the little brother of Seto Kaiba. Since their parents died at an early age, the two brothers are the only friend and family that either has. Mokuba idolizes Seto and sees only his good side. He is so devoted to his big brother that he automatically hates anyone who gets in his brother's way. At one point, Kaiba takes a sabbatical from heading up Kaiba Corporation, and gives Mokuba the key data for the corporation. Pegasus then kidnaps Mokuba to get the key data and takes him to the Duelist Kingdom.

"GRANDPA" SUGOROKU MUTOU

Yugi's grandfather, a former world traveler who owns a game store attached to Yugi's home, is a great game player. He knows everything there is to know about games and is especially well-versed in the ways of Duel Monsters. He teaches Yugi to believe in the heart of the cards. He also teaches Joey Wheeler how to be a better card game player. Pegasus J. Crawford steals his soul in order to get Yugi to come to the Duelist Kingdom tournament. It works.

ガズィデ
Weevil Underwood

(Japanese Name: Inspector Haga)

Weevil Underwood is the

RYOU BAKURA

Ryou Bakura is a school friend of Yugi's who possesses the rare and powerful Millennium Ring (which, among other things, has the power to detect other Millennium Items). The only problem is that whenever the magical Ring activates, Bakura can't seem to control its dark powers or its terribly dark hidden personality. He is a mysterious young man who has a passion for playing Duel Monsters that rivals even Yugi's and is seen by Téa Gardner several times (but she thinks it's just her mind, since he disappears soon after).

Ryou's Deck: Ryou calls his Deck an Occult Deck. It containes the Ouija Board, along with Dark Necrophia.

ガズィデ
Mako Tsunami

(Japanese Name: Ryouta Kajiki)

Mako is a jolly duelist, who makes his living by way of the sea. When he was young, his father was lost at sea, and Mako spends virtually all of his time looking for him.

Mako's Deck: Mako's Deck is composed of cards that have to do with the ocean. At first, his Deck appears to be only a plain Sea Deck. However, his Deck contains tricks and a special trump card. In the Duelist Kingdom, Mako uses the Leviathan as his big Monster. In Battle City, however he uses the Fortress Whale as his big Monster. Then, in a duel with Joey Wheeler, he reveals his trump card, the Legendary Fisherman (that can not be attacked while the Sea card is on the Field).

ガズィデ
"Bandit" Keith Howard

The extremely arrogant "Bandit" Keith earned that name when he won every major American prize-money tournament for Duel Monsters. Yet, he is not an official member of the tournament. Keith was disgraced and humiliated in front of millions of people by Pegasus, when Pegasus used a young boy to defeat him. Keith desperately desires to pay back that insult.

The Death Imitator

(Japanese Name: Player Killer)

The Industrial Illusion Company brought four Player Killers to the island in order to prevent people from winning the tournament by taking their Star Chips. This first Player Killer dressed up like Seto Kaiba, and used the deck that was stolen from Seto, in order to defeat Yugi.

Panik

(Japanese Name: Player Killer)

Panik is another Duelist that was brought to the island to get rid of competing Duelists. Yugi and company first meet him when they find out that Mai has lost all of her Star Chips to him. Yugi then promptly duels with him using darkness Monsters.

Bonz

(Japanese Name: Ghost Kotsuzuka)

"Bandit" Keith enlists the help of Bonz, along with two others, to get into Pegasus' castle.

Para and Dox

(Japanese Names: Mei and Kyuu)

Para and Dox are known as The Labyrinth Brothers, the Player Killers of the labyrinth, because the combined names of these characters in Japanese makes the word "Meikyuu," meaning maze or labyrinth. They face Yugi and Joey Wheeler in a Tag Duel.

THE CARD GAME

In Yu-Gi-Oh Duel Monsters, two players face off in an all-out battle, engaging in a Match consisting of three card battles called Duels. Although the game is fun whatever the skill level of the players, it takes practice, strategy and luck to emerge victorious from the Match, as there are many factors that players can manipulate to vanquish their foe. The main battles are waged between incredible Monsters split into 20 different types, each with their own unique skills and fighting styles. In addition, players can use magic, set traps, change the battlefield itself, and even fuse two Monsters together to form a Monster of immense power! Each card battle against an opponent in which a win, loss, or draw is determined is referred to as a Duel.

Each player begins a Duel with 8000 Life Points. Life Points decrease as a result of damage calculation after battle. There are three ways to win a Duel. First, whoever reduces the opponent's Life Points to 0, wins the Duel. Second, if a player's Deck runs out of cards during a Duel, the first player unable to draw a card loses. (Bearing this in mind, a good duelist should make every card count.) Third, if any player holds in his or her hand the right leg, left leg, right arm, and left arm of The Forbidden One cards, as well as an Exodia the Forbidden One card (5 cards in all), that player instantly wins the Duel.

The Deck used for dueling must contain a minimum of 40 cards. Aside from this minimum, a Deck can contain as many cards as a player likes. In addition to this Dueling Deck, a player can also have exactly 15 additional cards (no more, no less) in a separate pile known as the Side Deck. The Side Deck allows a player to modify the Dueling Deck to better suit his or her strategy during a Match. Between Duels, a player can exchange any card from the Side Deck with any card from the Dueling Deck—as long as the Dueling Deck ends up with the same number of cards that it began the Match with. In any Match, the Dueling Deck and the Side Deck combined cannot contain more than 3 copies of the same card. To begin, each player draws 5 cards from the top of their respective Dueling Decks. Once both players have 5 cards in their hands, the Duel (and the action-packed fun) begins.

THE ENGLISH— LANGUAGE CARD SETS

With two English-language starter decks (each composed of 50 cards), and the entire set of First Edition booster cards (124 in all) now available, there are a total of 224 cards that can be collected. Booster packs include eight common cards and one rare card. The First

Edition booster set consists of 82 common cards, 22 rare cards, 10 super-rare cards, and 10 ultra-rare cards. The two Starter Decks (a Yugi deck and a Kaiba deck) each contain Monster Cards, Magic Cards, Trap Cards, 3 Foil Cards, an Official Rule Book, and a Duel Field. To help you get your collection going, here is a checklist of all of the English-language cards presently available.

THE YUGI STARTER DECK

SDY-001	Mystical Elf
SDY-002	Feral Imp
SDY-003	Winged Dragon,Guardian of the Fortress #1
SDY-004	Summoned Skull
SDY-005	Beaver Warrior
SDY-006	Dark Magician
SDY-007	Gaia The Fierce Knight
SDY-008	Curse of Dragon
SDY-009	Celtic Guardian
SDY-010	Mammoth Graveyard
SDY-011	Great White
SDY-012	Silver Fang
SDY-013	Giant Soldier of Stone
SDY-014	Dragon Zombie
SDY-015	Doma The Angel of Silence
SDY-016	Ansatsu
SDY-017	Witty Phantom
SDY-018	Claw Reacher
SDY-019	Mystic Clown
SDY-020	Sword of Dark Destruction
SDY-021	Book of Secret Arts
SDY-022	Dark Hole
SDY-023	Dian Keto the Cure Master
SDY-024	Ancient Elf
SDY-025	Magical Ghost
SDY-026	Fissure
SDY-027	Trap Hole
SDY-028	Two-Pronged Attack
SDY-029	De-Spell
SDY-030	Monster Reborn
SDY-031	Reinforcements
SDY-032	Change of Heart
SDY-033	The Stern Mystic
SDY-034	Wall of Illusion
SDY-035	Neo the Magic Swordsman
SDY-036	Baron of the Fiend Sword
SDY-037	Man-Eating Treasure Chest
SDY-038	Sorcerer of the Doomed
SDY-039	Last Will
SDY-040	Waboku
SDY-041	Soul Exchange
SDY-042	Card Destruction
SDY-043	Trap Master
SDY-044	Dragon Capture Jar
SDY-045	Yami
SDY-046	Man-Eater Bug
SDY-047	Reverse Trap
SDY-048	Remove Trap
SDY-049	Castle Walls
SDY-050	Ultimate Offering

THE KAIBA STARTER DECK

SDK-001	Blue-Eyes White Dragon
SDK-002	Hitotsu-Me Giant
SDK-003	Ryu-Kishin
SDK-004	The Wicked Worm Beast
SDK-005	Battle Ox
SDK-006	Koumori Dragon
SDK-007	Judge Man
SDK-008	Rogue Doll
SDK-009	Kojikocy
SDK-010	Uraby
SDK-011	Gyakutenno Megami
SDK-012	Mystic Horseman
SDK-013	Terra the Terrible
SDK-014	Dark Titan of Terror
SDK-015	Dark Assassin
SDK-016	Master & Expert
SDK-017	Unknown Warrior of Fiend
SDK-018	Mystic Clown
SDK-019	Ogre of the Black Shadow
SDK-020	Dark Energy
SDK-021	Invigoration
SDK-022	Dark Hole
SDK-023	Ookazi
SDK-024	Ryu-Kishin Powered
SDK-025	Swordstalker
SDK-026	La Jinn the Mystical Genie of the Lamp
SDK-027	Rude Kaiser
SDK-028	Destroyer Golem
SDK-029	Skull Red Bird
SDK-030	D. Human
SDK-031	Pale Beast
SDK-032	Fissure
SDK-033	Trap Hole
SDK-034	Two-Pronged Attack
SDK-035	De-Spell
SDK-036	Monster Reborn
SDK-037	The Inexperienced Spy
SDK-038	Reinforcements
SDK-039	Ancient Telescope
SDK-040	Just Desserts
SDK-041	Lord of D.
SDK-042	The Flute of Summoning Dragon
SDK-043	Mysterious Puppeteer
SDK-044	Trap Master
SDK-045	Sogen
SDK-046	Hane-Hane
SDK-047	Reverse Trap
SDK-048	Remove Trap
SDK-049	Castle Walls
SDK-050	Ultimate Offering

THE FIRST EDITION BOOSTER SERIES

LOB-001 Blue-Eyes White Dragon

LOB-002 Hitotsu-Me Giant

LOB-007 Celtic Guardian

LOB-008 Basic Insect

LOB-009 Mammoth Graveyard

LOB-010 Silver Fang

LOB-011 Dark Gray

LOB-012 Trial of Hell

LOB-013 Nemuriko

LOB-014 The 13th Grave

LOB-015 Charubin the Fire Knight

LOB-016 Flame Manipulator

LOB-017 **Monster Egg**

LOB-018 **Firegrass**

LOB-019 **Darkfire Dragon**

LOB-020 **Dark King of the Abyss**

LOB-021 **Fiend Reflection #2**

LOB-022 **Fusionist**

LOB-023 **Turtle Tiger**

LOB-024 **Petit Dragon**

LOB-025 **Petit Angel**

LOB-026 **Hinotama Soul**

LOB-027 **Aqua Madoor**

LOB-028 **Kagemusha of the Blue Flame**

LOB-029 **Flame Ghost**

LOB-030 **Two-Mouth Darkruler**

LOB-031 **Dissolverock**

LOB-032 **Root Water**

THE FURIOUS SEA KING

[AQUA]
Grand King of the Seven Seas, he's able to summon massive tidal waves to down the enemy.

ATK/ 800 DEF/ 700

LOB-033 The Furious Sea King

GREEN PHANTOM KING

[PLANT]
This youthful king of the forests lives in a green world, abundant with trees and wildlife.

ATK/ 500 DEF/1600

LOB-034 Green Phantom King

RAY & TEMPERATURE

[FAIRY]
The Sun and the North Wind join hands to deliver a devastating combination of heat and gale-force winds.

ATK/1000 DEF/1000

LOB-035 Ray & Temperature

KING FOG

[FIEND]
A fiend that dwells in a blinding curtain of smoke.

ATK/1000 DEF/ 900

LOB-036 King Fog

MYSTICAL SHEEP #2

[BEAST]
A monstrous sheep with a long tail for hypnotizing enemies.

ATK/ 800 DEF/1000

LOB-037 Mystical Sheep #2

MASAKI THE LEGENDARY SWORDSMAN

[WARRIOR]
Legendary swordmaster Masaki is a veteran of over 100 battles.

ATK/1100 DEF/1100

LOB-038 Masaki the Legendary Swordsman

KURAMA

[WINGED BEAST]
A vicious bird that attacks from the skies with its whip-like tail.

ATK/ 800 DEF/ 800

LOB-039 Kurama

BEAST FANGS
[MAGIC CARD]

A Beast-Type monster equipped with this card increases its ATK and DEF by 300 points.

LOB-041 Beast Fangs

VIOLET CRYSTAL
[MAGIC CARD]

A Zombie-Type monster equipped with this card increases its ATK and DEF by 300 points.

LOB-042 Violet Crystal

BOOK OF SECRET ARTS
[MAGIC CARD]

A Spellcaster-Type monster equipped with this card increases its ATK and DEF by 300 points.

LOB-043 Book of Secret Arts

POWER OF KAISHIN
[MAGIC CARD]

An Aqua-Type monster equipped with this card increases its ATK and DEF by 300 points.

LOB-044 Power of Kaishin

DRAGON CAPTURE JAR
[TRAP CARD]

All Dragon-Type monsters on the field are switched to Defense Position and remain in this position as long as this card is active.

LOB-045 Dragon Capture Jar

FOREST
[MAGIC CARD]

Increases the ATK and DEF of all Insect, Beast, Plant, and Beast-Warrior-Type monsters by 200 points.

LOB-046 Forest

WASTELAND
[MAGIC CARD]

Increases the ATK and DEF of all Dinosaur, Zombie, and Rock-Type monsters by 200 points.

LOB-047 Wasteland

MOUNTAIN
[MAGIC CARD]

Increases the ATK and DEF of all Dragon, Winged Beast, and Thunder-Type monsters by 200 points.

LOB-048 Mountain

SOGEN
[MAGIC CARD]

Increases the ATK and DEF of all Beast-Warrior and Warrior-Type monsters by 200 points.

LOB-049 Sogen

UMI
[MAGIC CARD]

Increases the ATK and DEF of all Fish, Sea Serpent, Thunder, and Aqua-Type monsters by 200 points. Also decreases the ATK and DEF of all Machine and Pyro-Type monsters by 200 points.

LOB-050 **Umi**

YAMI
[MAGIC CARD]

Increases the ATK and DEF of all Fiend and Spellcaster-Type monsters by 200 points. Also decreases the ATK and DEF of all Fairy-Type monsters by 200 points.

LOB-051 **Yami**

DARK HOLE
[MAGIC CARD]

Destroys all monsters on the field.

LOB-052 **Dark Hole**

RAIGEKI
[MAGIC CARD]

Destroys all of your opponent's monsters on the field.

LOB-053 **Raigeki**

RED MEDICINE
[MAGIC CARD]

Increases your Life Points by 500 points.

LOB-054 **Red Medicine**

SPARKS
[MAGIC CARD]

Inflicts 200 points of Direct Damage to your opponent's Life Points.

LOB-055 **Sparks**

HINOTAMA
[MAGIC CARD]

Inflicts 500 points of Direct Damage to your opponent's Life Points.

LOB-056 **Hinotama**

FISSURE
[MAGIC CARD]

Destroys opponent's face-up monster with the lowest ATK.

LOB-057 **Fissure**

TRAP HOLE
[TRAP CARD]

If the ATK of a monster summoned by your opponent (excluding Special Summoned) is 1000 points or more, the monster is destroyed.

LOB-058 **Trap Hole**

REMOVE TRAP
[MAGIC CARD]

Destroys 1 face-up Trap Card on the field.

LOB-060 **Remove Trap**

MYSTICAL ELF

[SPELLCASTER]
A delicate elf that lacks offense, but has a terrific defense backed by mystical power.

ATK/ 800 DEF/2000

LOB-062 **Mystical Elf**

TYHONE

[WINGED BEAST]
Capable of firing cannonballs from its mouth for long-range attacks, this creature is particularly effective in mountain battles.

ATK/1200 DEF/1400

LOB-063 **Tyhone**

BEAVER WARRIOR

[BEAST-WARRIOR]
What this creature lacks in size it makes up for in defense when battling in the prairie.

ATK/1200 DEF/1500

LOB-064 **Beaver Warrior**

GRAVEDIGGER GHOUL
[MAGIC CARD]

Select 2 Monster Cards from your opponent's Graveyard. These Monster Cards are removed from play for the remainder of the Duel.

LOB-065 **Gravedigger Ghoul**

KARBONALA WARRIOR

[WARRIOR / FUSION]
"M-Warrior #1" + "M-Warrior #2"

ATK/1500 DEF/1200

LOB-067 **Karbonala Warrior**

GIANT SOLDIER OF STONE

[ROCK]
A giant warrior made of stone. A punch from this creature has earth-shaking results.

ATK/1300 DEF/2000

LOB-068 **Giant Soldier of Stone**

LOB-069 **Uraby**

LOB-072 **Witty Phantom**

LOB-073 **Larvas**

LOB-074 **Hard Armor**

LOB-075 **Man Eater**

LOB-076 **M-Warrior #1**

LOB-077 **M-Warrior #2**

LOB-078 **Spirit of the Harp**

LOB-079 **Armaill**

LOB-080 **Terra the Terrible**

LOB-081 **Frenzied Panda**

LOB-082 **Kumootoko**

LOB-083 **Meda Bat**

LOB-084 **Enchanting Mermaid**

LOB-085 **Fireyarou**

LOB-086 **Dragoness the Wicked Knight**

LOB-087 **One-Eyed Shield Dragon**	LOB-088 **Dark Energy**	LOB-089 **Laser Cannon Armor**	LOB-091 **Silver Bow and Arrow**

LOB-092 **Dragon Treasure**	LOB-093 **Electro-Whip**	LOB-094 **Mystical Moon**	LOB-095 **Stop Defense**

LOB-096 **Machine Conversion Factory**	LOB-098 **Follow Wind**	LOB-100 **Final Flame**	LOB-101 **Swords of Revealing Light**

LOB-102 **Metal Dragon**	LOB-103 **Spike Seadra**	LOB-105 **Skull Red Bird**	LOB-107 **Flower Wolf**

LOB-109 **Sand Stone**   LOB-110 **Hane-Hane**   LOB-111 **Misairuzame**   LOB-112 **Steel Ogre Grotto #1**

LOB-113 **Lesser Dragon**   LOB-114 **Darkworld Thorns**   LOB-115 **Drooling Lizard**   LOB-116 **Armored Starfish**

LOB-117 **Succubus Knight**   LOB-119 **Pot of Greed**

THE FIRST EDITION
BOOSTER SERIES

THE CARDS

Three main card types are used in the Yu-Gi-Oh Game: Monster Cards, Magic Cards, and Trap Cards. Each type of card is divided into further sub-categories, each of which has a special role in the game. Here are the different type of cards and how to read them.

MONSTER CARDS

A Monster Card is the basic card used to attack your opponent. Monster Cards are categorized by Type and Attribute. There are 20 different Types and 6 different Attributes. Type and Attribute affect each monster's ability to Attack and Defend. The overall strength of a monster is indicated by its Level (the number of stars at the upper right of the Monster Card). Normal and Fusion Monster Cards are color-coded YELLOW. They look like this:

Monster Name

Attribute

Level

Type

ATK (attack points)

DEF (defense points)

Card Description

AQUA MADOOR

1st Edition   LOB-027

[SPELLCASTER]
A wizard of the waters that conjures a liquid wall to crush any enemies that oppose him.

ATK/1200 DEF/2000

85639257   ©1996 KAZUKI TAKAHASHI

There are four kinds of Monster Cards:

Normal, Fusion, Ritual and Effect. The types and attributes of each are:

Normal Monster Cards

—The types of Normal Monster Cards are: Dragon • Spellcaster • Zombie • Warrior • Beast-Warrior • Beast • Winged Beast • Fiend • Fairy • Insect • Dinosaur • Reptile Fish • Sea Serpent • Machine • Thunder • Aqua • Pyro • Rock • Plant. Each can have any of the following Attributes: Earth, Fire, Light, Water, Wind, Dark.

ガ ズ ィ デ ダ ヂ ド ジ バ エ

Fusion Monster Cards

—Fusion means using 2 or more Monster Cards (together with the Magic Card Polymerization) to create a new monster, represented by a Fusion Monster Card. Each Fusion Monster Card lists the monsters necessary to create it (Fusion-Material Monsters), and is further identified as Fusion next to its Type. The color of a Fusion Monster Card is Violet. A Fusion Deck is a group of Fusion Monster Cards that result from a successful Fusion.

ガ ズ ィ デ ダ ヂ ド ジ バ エ

Ritual Monster Cards

—These are not yet available, but will be in the near future. They offer an exciting twist to game play because they are special monsters that can be summoned onto the field only when a player has a designated Ritual Magic Card and the Monster Cards required to fulfill the conditions described on the Ritual Magic Card as a Tribute. Ritual Monster Cards are special color-coded blue.

ガ ズ ィ デ ダ ヂ ド ジ バ エ

Effect Monster Cards

—Monster Cards that possess magical effects are referred to as Effect Monster Cards. The broad range of Effects are divided into various types. Effect Monster Cards are color-coded orange.

magic CARDS

Magic Cards are cards that affect other cards, players or the game field. There is a combined limit of 5 Magic Cards and Trap Cards (described later) on the Duel Field for each player at any time. There are several types of Magic Cards, all of which are identified by the card icons that appear in the upper right corner of the card. Magic cards are color-coded GREEN.

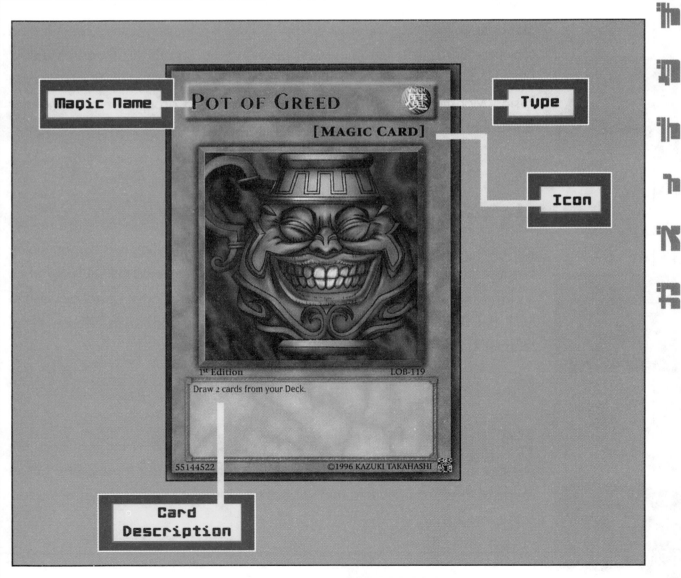

Magic Name

Type

[MAGIC CARD]

Icon

Card Description

POT OF GREED

1st Edition   LOB-119

Draw 2 cards from your Deck.

55144522   ©1996 KAZUKI TAKAHASHI

The Types of Magic Cards are:

Normal Magic Cards

Normal Magic Cards—Once their magic is activated these cards are destroyed. They are often very powerful.

Continuous Magic Cards

Continuous Magic Cards—These cards remain on the field once they are played and their magic effect continues until they are destroyed or removed. There is often a cost involved to maintain the effect of this type of Magic Card.

Equip Magic Cards

Equip Magic Cards—These cards allow a player to modify the strength of monsters. A player may equip either his or her own or the opponent's Monster Cards with Equip Magic Cards. In some cases, certain monsters cannot be equipped with these cards; however one monster can be equipped with several Equip Magic Cards. [Note: Equip Magic Cards, even cards attached to an opponent's Monster, count toward the 5-card Magic & Trap Card limit, so a player needs to be sure to use them wisely].

Field Magic Cards

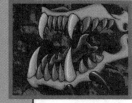

Field Magic Cards—These cards are used to alter the conditions on the field and modify the Attack and Defense capabilities of monsters. They are not included in the Magic & Trap Zone's 5-card limit. There can only be 1 active Field Magic Card on the field at any given time between both players. When a new Field Magic Card is activated, the previous active card is sent to the Graveyard. If a Field Magic Card is destroyed and there are no active Field Magic Cards on the field, the field returns to the original state that it was in at the beginning of the game.

Quick-Play Magic Cards

Quick-Play Magic Cards—These types of Magic Cards are not yet available, but will be in future Yu-Gi-Oh releases.

Ritual Magic Cards

Ritual Magic Cards—These types of Magic Cards also are not yet available, but will be included in future Yu-Gi-Oh releases. These cards are necessary to summon a Ritual Monster. After the Ritual Monster is summoned, it is destroyed together with the required Tribute monster(s).

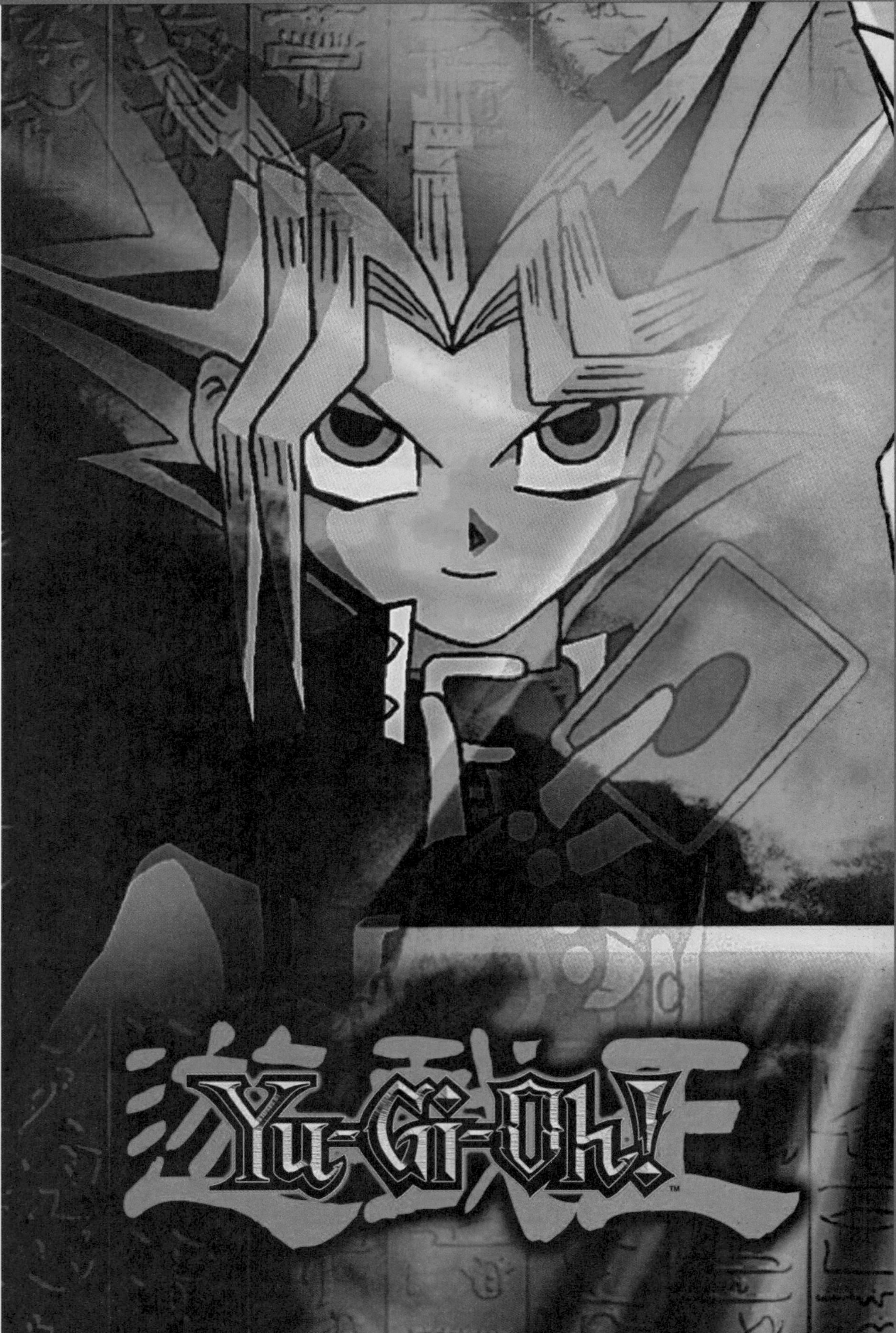
Yu-Gi-Oh!

trap CARDS

These are cards that are normally played face down, and do not become activated until they are flipped face-up (which can be done at any time after the start of an opponent's turn). Trap Card types are identified by the card icons that appear in the upper right corner of the card. Trap Cards are color-coded PURPLE.

The types of Trap Cards are:

Normal Trap Cards—A normal Trap Card has no icon. Once activated, this type of card is destroyed.

Continuous Trap Cards—These cards remain on the field once they are activated and their effect continues until they are destroyed or removed. There is often a cost involved to maintain the effect of this type of Trap Card.

Counter Trap Cards—This type of Trap Card is not yet available, but will be included in future Yu-Gi-Oh releases. These Trap Cards are activated in response to the summons of monsters, or to neutralize the effects of Magic or Trap Cards. Once activated, this type of card is destroyed.

Type

Trap Name

Icon

Card Description

DRAGON CAPTURE JAR 罠

[TRAP CARD ∞]

1st Edition   LOB-045

All Dragon-Type monsters on the field are switched to Defense Position and remain in this position as long as this card is active.

50045299   ©1996 KAZUKI TAKAHASHI

DECK CONSTRUCTION
TIPS AND HINTS

One of the most interesting aspects of the Yu-Gi-Oh Card Game is constructing a personal deck. Because of the almost limitless combinations of cards, and their interaction with each other, card deck construction becomes a vital part of Dueling. Here are some basic hints and tips to follow in constructing your Deck.

Although there is no maximum limit to the number of cards that can be in a deck (a deck must contain a minimum of 40 cards), decks with too many cards mean a player will have less of a chance of drawing the cards he or she needs, so it's best to limit a Dueling Deck to approximately 40 cards.

The building blocks of all Decks are the Monster Cards. No matter how many powerful Magic or Trap Cards a player has, no Monsters on the field means the player has nothing to defend his or her Life Points with. A general rule of thumb is that roughly half of a Deck should be made up of Monsters.

In order to perform a Tribute Summon (required for a Level 5 or higher monster), one or two Monsters must be offered (i.e., sacrificed to the Graveyard) as a Tribute. If a Deck is filled with high-level Monsters, summoning them to the field will be very costly. Instead, include lots of Level 4 or lower monsters in your Deck and keep the number of high-level monsters to a minimum.

Effect Monsters with Magic or Trap effects play an important strategic role in Duels. A powerful Deck can be created that takes full advantage of these effects. For example, the Hane-Hane card forces an opponent to return one Monster from the field to his or her hand. Using this card at the right moment could leave an opponent's Life Points wide open for an attack from a high-level Monster. The point is that these cards should be carefully considered for inclusion in a Deck.

In a Duel, only 1 card can be drawn during the Draw Phase. Therefore, you should include cards in your deck (like Pot Of Greed) that increase your chances of drawing vital cards from your deck, or permit you to draw more cards than your opponent.

In between Duels, you are allowed to use a Side Deck of 15 cards to adjust the contents of your Deck. This can be of critical importance during a Duel. Prepare your Side Deck with cards that help address the weaknesses in your Deck or have the power to neutralize specific cards.

THE DUEL FIELD

Every card that a player plays or discards will be placed on the Duel Field. The Duel Field shows where to place and discard the cards that are brought into and out of play during a Match.

Konami of America recently released two new video games based on the ultra-successful Yu-Gi-Oh animated series: Yu-Gi-Oh Dark Duel Stories for Nintendo Game Boy® Color and Yu-Gi-Oh Forbidden Memories for Sony PlayStation®. Konami has announced its plan to release games for next generation consoles later in 2002, including PlayStation® 2 and Game Boy® Advance. According to Dick Wnuk (COO for Konami of America), the already available Yu-Gi-Oh video games "offer kids a rich world that they themselves can conquer through strategic thinking, puzzle solving and clever card combinations."

The adventures begin in Yu-Gi-Oh Dark Duel Stories for Game Boy® Color as players compete to become the strongest duelist in the world. Battling for cards and experience in the Duel Monsters card game, players must think strategically to craft their customized 40-card deck. In order to gain cards, players can win battles, import cards by inputting passwords found on the Official Trading Cards, trade with friends using a link-cable, or even create new cards using the construction feature.

THE VIDEO GAMES

In Yu-Gi-Oh Forbidden Memories for PlayStation®, players voyage to ancient Egypt and embark on an adventure to save the world from total destruction! It is only the young pharaoh who can unlock the mysteries of the Shadow Game and the Seven Magical Totems! Players must duel with the townspeople to decipher clues and solve puzzles in an effort to avert the kingdom's imminent doom.

Any way you look at it, the already available Yu-Gi-Oh video games are fun and challenging and are already high on the list of must-have games.

THE TELEVISION ANIMATED SERIES

The Yu-Gi-Oh animated television series is in full swing, now having been expanded to six days per week on the Kids' WB Channel. For those of you who may have missed any episodes, here is a synopsis of the first 10 episodes.

Episode 1: The Chill of Blue Eyes White Dragon

This episode introduces almost all of the major characters. Yugi and Jounouchi are playing Duel Monsters at school, with Anzu and Honda watching. After school, Yugi says that he can get his grandfather, Sugoroku, to show them a super-rare card, so they all go to Yugi's house where his grandfather shows them the Blue Eyes White Dragon card (only four of which exist in the world). Kaiba then comes into the store and offers a case full of cards for the rare card, which Sugoroku turns down. Kaiba then forces Sugoroku into a Duel, during which he tears up Sugoroku's Blue Eyes White Dragon. Sugoroku then gives Yugi his deck of cards and asks Yugi to Duel. Yugi accepts, but starts to get annihilated when one of Kaiba's Blue Eyes comes out. When Kaiba plays his second Blue Eyes, Yugi draws and plays the Sealing Swords of Light to buy some time; but it is only a temporary fix. Then, Yugi sees a vision of Sugoroku, who tells him that the cards in his hand are pieces of a puzzle that can be used to summon the great Exodia. After Kaiba's third Blue Eyes comes out, Yugi draws the final piece for Exodia, completing the set of five and winning the game.

Episode 2: Illusionist No Face's Trap

Another game is being played at school between Jounouchi and Anzu. Anzu wins easily and Jounouchi starts to get depressed. Yugi tells him that his Deck needs to be composed of a combination of Monster and Magic cards and Jounouchi asks Yugi to teach him how to play better. Yugi takes him to Sugoroku's store, where Sugoroku offers to start teaching Jounouchi. Some time later in the month, Yugi and company are watching a Duel between Inspector Haga and Dinosaur Ryuzaki at the Japanese Duel Monsters tournament on television. Haga wins. Sugoroku then gives Yugi a package with a videotape in it. They play the tape and see Pegasus J. Crawford introduce himself, and use the power of his Millennium Eye to freeze everyone but Yugi. Pegasus then tells Yugi that he will play a game with him for fifteen minutes, at the end of which time the person with the highest Life Points will win. As the Duel progresses, Yugi comes to the conclusion that Pegasus can read his mind. Yugi thinks he has the battle won, but a trick card from Pegasus takes Yugi's Life Points to lower than his, and Pegasus wins. Pegasus then asks Yugi to be in the Duelist Kingdom tournament. Yugi is about to refuse, but Pegasus steals Sugoroku's soul, forcing Yugi to come to the Duelist Kingdom.

Episode 3: The Loss of Exodia

Yugi has made up his mind to go to the Duelist Kingdom. Jounouchi gets a videotape from his sister. On his way home from school, Yugi finds an envelope with four special cards in it. The next day at school, Yugi and company are considering the cards. One indicates that there will be a large amount of prize money given to the winner of the Duelist Kingdom tournament. Jounouchi takes special interest in that card. The next evening, Yugi goes to the boat dock to leave for the Duelist Kingdom, and sees Jounouchi being denied boarding onto the boat because he doesn't have any Star Chips (needed for a person to enter the tournament). Yugi gives him one.

Meanwhile, Anzu and Honda are trying to get onto the boat also. On the boat, Yugi and Jounochi run into Mai Kujaku, Inspector Haga and Dinosaur Ryuzaki. Haga asks to see the Exodia cards that Yugi defeated Kaiba with, then he tosses them overboard. Jounouchi dives in after them, then Yugi follows. They are saved by Anzu and Honda. Jounouchi then tells them that he wants to go the Duelist Kingdom to win the tournament and get enough money for an operation to save his sister's eyesight.

Episode 4: Inspector Combo

Yugi and friends arrive at the Duelist Kingdom, where Pegasus explains the rules of the tournament. In a duel, players will bet Star Chips. Those who have ten can get into Pegasus' castle. Those who lose all of their Star Chips will be expelled from the tournament. Yugi and Haga begin their duel. Haga bets two Star Chips. Even though Yugi has only one Star Chip, he bets his deck against Haga's other Chip. Early in the duel, Haga tries to surprise Yugi with a new rule (that is used in the Kingdom) which increases a monster's power if it matches the terrain. This proves fruitless, as Yugi has already figured it out. However, Yugi is surprised by the fact that monsters that match the terrain cancel out effects on those that don't match the terrain. When Haga plays his deadliest combo, the Basic Insect Combo, Yugi can't attack or he'll be destroyed by the combo. Eventually, Yugi places a card, and when Haga attacks, Yugi activates the card, Holy Barrier-Mirror Force, reflecting the attack back at all of Haga's Monsters.

ガ ズ イ デ

Episode 5: Perfectly Evolved Great Moth

Yugi has just reflected back Haga's attack, destroying all of his Monsters, and doing a lot of damage to his Life Points. Anzu remarks that the game will be a piece of cake, but Mai steps in and states otherwise. Haga announces that he has a trump card that will be coming soon. He plays a Monster, but Yugi doesn't attack, since Haga still has a card placed on the Field. Yugi then plays Monster Recall, bringing his Monsters back to his hand, and giving him a new hand of five cards. He plays Kuribo and attacks, activating Haga's Parasite Worm, getting rid of it, but destroying Kuribo in the process. Haga laughs, telling him that the game has progressed according to plan. He then plays the Evolutionary Cocoon card on his Monster, the Larva Moth, and tells Yugi that the Perfectly Evolved Great Moth will appear in five turns, and will defeat him. Yugi tries to attack the Cocoon with Dark Knight Gaia, but with the Field Power Source, the Cocoon's defense strength is too high. Yugi then plays another Monster. The turns pass by, but taking a hint from Jounouchi, Yugi summons Curse of Dragon, and plays Scorched Earth to burn away the forest under the Cocoon, lowering the defense strength. Yugi attacks the Cocoon, but it's too late to stop the Great Moth from coming out. Haga's Great Moth flies, and just before it attacks, Yugi plays a card. Ruiz is destroyed, along with Dark Knight Gaia. Or so he thinks. Yugi plays the Fusion card, combining Curse of Dragon and Dark Knight Gaia into Dragon Knight Gaia. Their attack strengths are equal at first, but Haga reveals that the attack of the Great Moth spreads poison pollen, which continually decreases Gaia's attack strength. Yugi plays the Demon Rain card to wash the pollen off, soaking all of the Monsters in play, but it is not enough, as the attack strength of Gaia is low enough for the Moth to destroy it. Yugi is left with very few Life Points. Yugi laughs, stating that Gaia was just bait. He then summons Demon Summon. Since the Demon has an electrical attack, and the Great Moth is soaked, the Demon's attack strength is increased. The Demon handily toasts the Moth, and wins the Match for Yugi. Haga is removed from the tournament, and Jounouchi takes Haga's duel glove.

Episode 6: Magnificent Harpy Lady

With the battle with Haga out of the way, it's Jounouchi's turn to Duel, but the group runs into Mai Kujaku. Mai challenges Jounouchi. He starts the battle with Mai, but her Harpy Lady proves to be too much of a problem since it matches up with the mountain terrain and can fly, thus eliminating the Field Power Source on the enemy monsters when they attack. Jounouchi's Monsters are cut down, but with some advice from Yugi, Jounouchi brings out the Baby Dragon. Mai plays Ten-Thousand Reflections, multiplying her Harpy Lady into three. Jounouchi finally draws the Time Magician card and uses it to turn the Baby Dragon into the Millennium Dragon. It ages Mai's Harpy Ladies, and one swift hit from the Millennium Dragon's Millennium Nose Breath incinerates them, giving the Match to Jounouchi.

Episode 7: The God of the Sea, Leviathan

Yugi and friends go looking for food. Jounouchi smells something, and takes off in a different direction. The others find some fish cooking, but no one seems to be around. Jounouchi and Honda are about to take the fish when Ryouta Kajiki comes out of the water, demanding the fish back. When he realizes Yugi is among the group, he allows them to eat. When they finish, Kajiki challenges Yugi to a Duel, which Yugi accepts. Starting the duel on the sea, Yugi can't see the first Monster that Kajiki has played because it is under the water. Yugi tries to attack in various ways, but is unable to, and succumbs to Kajiki's Sea Stealth Attack. Yugi plays a Silver Fang, then the Full Moon card to enhance the monster. Kajiki brings out Leviathan, and turns Yugi's side of the Field almost completely into water, with only one place to play Monsters. He summons a Rock Soldier in defense mode. Kajiki carelessly surrounds Yugi's Monster with all of his own. Yugi puts the Rock Soldier into attack mode, and then attacks the Moon card above the Field. The water from Yugi's side recedes, exposing all of Kajiki's monsters. Yugi summons Curse of Dragon and plays Scorched Earth, annihilates all of Kajiki's Monsters, and wins the Duel. Kajiki thanks Yugi for the Duel, and then jumps into the sea again.

ガズィデガズデガズ

Episode 8: Stolen Blue Eyes White Dragon

At Pegasus' castle, someone makes his way out of the window with the help of a rope. After the Duel with Kajiki, the group runs into a boy being taken away by Pegasus' henchman. They try to rescue him but fail, and the henchman explains that all of the boy's Star Chips were lost. The boy then tells them that they were stolen, along with his cards. After chasing both the boy and the henchman to the departing boat, Yugi tells him that they'll track down the person who stole them. At the duel ring in the field, the thief (who turns out to be Mokuba) shows up and challenges Yugi to a Duel. Pegasus is after the Kaiba Corporation for some reason, and (as Mokuba explains what he overheard), if Pegasus can get Yugi to lose the tournament, the Big Five of the Kaiba Corporation will take the company from the now-absent Kaiba, and give it to Pegasus. Yugi convinces Mokuba that he will defeat Pegasus, and that he should give back the Star Chips and cards he stole. Back at the dock, the ship has already left and the henchman grabs Mokuba. Yugi challenges the man to a Duel, but he won't Duel, explaining that there is a special opponent in mind for Yugi. When they return to the duel ring, they find Kaiba standing there.

Episode 9: Rise From the Grave! Magical Silk Hat

Pegasus' henchman reveals that it is not Kaiba that is standing there, but Kaiba's ghost, who died as a result of his grudge against Yugi. Yugi refuses to believe it, but decides to Duel anyway. Kaiba starts out with the same Monster he did in the earlier battle (a Cyclops), but Yugi brings out the Black Magician and destroys it. Then, Kaiba brings out a Blue Eyes White Dragon. Meanwhile, the real Seto Kaiba makes his way into his mansion, which is now surrounded with Pegasus' guards. The Kaiba-ghost decides not to attack, but instead places a card in defense mode. Yugi puts his Monsters in defense mode, and plays a Curse of Dragon in defense mode. Kaiba then activates his card, Defense Seal, turning all of Yugi's Monsters to attack mode, and prevents him from playing further Monsters in defense mode. He then destroys the Curse of Dragon. Kaiba tries to hack into the main computer of the Industrial Illusion Company to find out what is going on. Remembering his vow to Mokuba, Yugi believes that Kaiba is really alive, and plays the Magical Silk Hat card, hiding his Black Magician in one of four Silk Hats. Yugi goads the fake Kaiba into attacking and the Burst Stream flies at one of the Silk Hats.

Episode 10: Blue Eyes White Dragon's Counterattack!

The fake Kaiba's Burst Stream hits the wrong one. Yugi looks smug and places a card on the field, being hidden in one of the three remaining Hats. He tells Kaiba that one of them has a Trap card in it. Kaiba attacks and hits the one with the Trap card, the Hexagram Curse. Blue Eyes White Dragon is prevented from attacking, and its attack strength is reduced. Yugi then attacks with the Black Magician, destroying Blue Eyes. Before he has time to savor the victory, however, the fake Kaiba brings out another Blue Eyes and destroys the Black Magician. Meanwhile, the real Kaiba has broken into the company's main computer, and finds that he has to help Yugi in order to save his own company. He begins to upload a virus to the Blue Eyes. Yugi has no choice but to play a Gremlin in attack mode. The fake Kaiba is about to end the battle when Blue Eyes begins to glow, and even though it attacks, its fails, and disappears. It is then revealed that the Kaiba is a fake, and is really the Death Imitator with a new shape. It keeps playing monsters in defense mode, until Yugi finally brings out the Holy Elf card, and enhances it with the Tome of Secrets Magic card. The Imitator draws the final Blue Eyes and attacks, but Yugi reflects the attack back with Mirror Force, which is in turn negated by the Attack Nullification card. Yugi finally plays the Raise Dead card, bringing one of the fake Kaiba's Blue Eyes back into play, and then with the power of the Holy Elf's chanting, annihilates the Imitator's Blue Eyes, winning the Match. After the battle, Yugi and friends realize that Mokuba is gone.

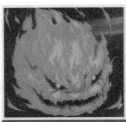

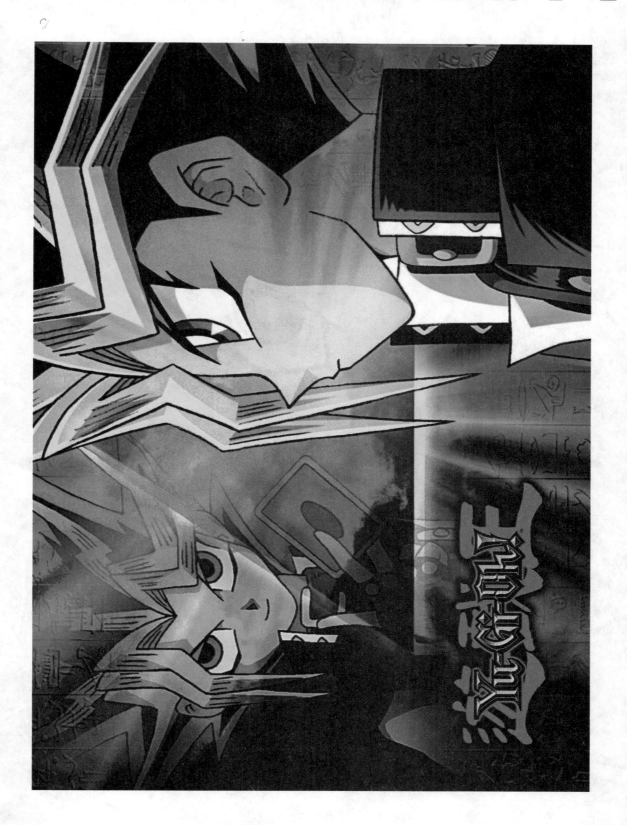

THE NEW METAL RAIDERS EXPANSION SERIES

THE HOT NEW METAL RAIDERS EXPANSION SET

Metal Raiders is an awesome expansion set. With its release, the game now takes on a more skill-oriented outcome. The ball is now in the court of the more skilled player, and the luck factor has been greatly reduced. Here are the cards.

MRD-000 Gate Guardian

MRD-001 Feral Imp

MRD-002 Winged Dragon, GOF#1

MRD-003 Summoned Skull

MRD-004 Rock Ogre Grotto #1

MRD-005 Armored Lizard

MRD-006 Killer Needle

MRD-007 Larve Moth

MRD-008 Harpie Lady

MRD-009 Harpie Lady Sisters

KOJIKOCY

[WARRIOR]
A man-hunter with powerful arms that can crush boulders.

ATK/1500 DEF/1200

MRD-010 Kojikocy

COCOON OF EVOLUTION

[INSECT / EFFECT]
You may treat this card as an Equip Magic Card on a favorable "Petit Moth" on the field. When equipped, the ATK and DEF of Petit Moth increases the same as "Cocoon of Evolution".

ATK/ 0 DEF/2000

MRD-011 Cocoon of Evolution

CRAWLING DRAGON

[DRAGON]
This weakened dragon can no longer fly, but is still a deadly force to be reckoned with.

ATK/1600 DEF/1400

MRD-012 Crawling Dragon

ARMORED ZOMBIE

[ZOMBIE]
This warrior blindly swings a deadly blade with devastating force.

ATK/1500 DEF/ 0

MRD-013 Armored Zombie

MASK OF DARKNESS

[FIEND / EFFECT]
FLIP: Select 1 Trap Card from your Graveyard and return it to your hand.

ATK/ 900 DEF/ 400

MRD-014 Mask of Darkness

DOMA THE ANGEL OF SILENCE

[FAIRY]
This fairy rules over the end of existence.

ATK/1600 DEF/1400

MRD-015 Doma the Angel of Silence

WHITE MAGICAL HAT

[SPELLCASTER / EFFECT]
When this card inflicts damage to your opponent's Life Points, 1 card must be discarded randomly from your opponent's hand to the Graveyard.

ATK/1000 DEF/ 700

MRD-016 White Magical Hat

BIG EYE

[FIEND / EFFECT]
FLIP: See the 5 cards from the top of your Deck, arrange them in any order desired, and replace them on top of the Deck.

ATK/1200 DEF/1000

MRD-017 Big Eye

MASKED SORCERER

[SPELLCASTER / EFFECT]
When you inflict damage to your opponent's Life Points with this card, draw 1 card from your Deck.

ATK/ 900 DEF/1400

MRD-019 Masked Sorcerer

ROARING OCEAN SNAKE

[AQUA / FUSION]
"Mystic Lamp" + "Hyosube"

ATK/2100 DEF/1800

MRD-020 Roaring Ocean Snake

WATER OMOTICS

[AQUA]
Transforms the water overflowing from a jar into attacking dragons.

ATK/1400 DEF/1200

MRD-021 Water Omotics

GROUND ATTACKER BUGROTH

[MACHINE]
A surface battle-robot that was once used for sea warfare.

ATK/1500 DEF/1000

MRD-022 Ground Attacker Bugroth

PETIT MOTH

[INSECT]
This small but deadly creature is better off avoided.

ATK/ 300 DEF/ 200

MRD-023 Petit Moth

ELEGANT EGOTIST

[MAGIC CARD]

When there are 1 or more "Harpie Lady" cards on the field, you can Special Summon 1 "Harpie Lady" or "Harpie Lady Sisters" card from your hand or your Deck.

MRD-024 Elegant Egotist

SUIJIN

[AQUA / EFFECT]
Reduce the ATK of an opponent's monster attacking this card to 0. This effect can be used only once. The card's owner chooses when to activate this effect.

ATK/2500 DEF/2400

MRD-027 Suijin

MYSTIC LAMP

[SPELLCASTER / EFFECT]
This monster may attack your opponent's Life Points directly.

ATK/ 400 DEF/ 300

MRD-028 Mystic Lamp

STEEL SCORPION

[MACHINE / EFFECT]
A non Machine-Type Monster attacking "Steel Scorpion" will be destroyed at the End Phase of your opponent's next turn after the attack.

ATK/ 250 DEF/ 300

MRD-029 Steel Scorpion

OCUBEAM

[FAIRY]
Frightening in appearance, this creature uses its large eyes and ears to keep track of any movement.

ATK/1550 DEF/1650

MRD-030 Ocubeam

OOGUCHI

[AQUA / EFFECT]
This monster may attack your opponent's Life Points directly.

ATK/ 300 DEF/ 250

MRD-032 Ooguchi

LEOGUN

[BEAST]
Huge monster with a lion's mane similar to the King of Beasts.

ATK/1750 DEF/1550

MRD-033 Leogun

BLAST JUGGLER

[MACHINE / EFFECT]
Offer this card as a Tribute during your Standby Phase if face-up to destroy a face-up monsters with an ATK of 1000 or less.

ATK/ 800 DEF/ 900

MRD-034 Blast Juggler

JINZO #7

[MACHINE / EFFECT]
This monster may attack your opponent's Life Points directly.

ATK/ 500 DEF/ 400

MRD-035 Jinzo #7

ANCIENT ELF

[SPELLCASTER]
This elf is rumored to have lived for thousands of years. He leads an army of spirits against his enemies.

ATK/1450 DEF/1200

MRD-037 Ancient Elf

DEEPSEA SHARK

[FISH / FUSION]
"Bottom Dweller" + "Tongyo"

ATK/1900 DEF/1600

MRD-038 Deepsea Shark

BOTTOM DWELLER

[FISH]
This is one sea creature whose wrath is something monsters fear to face.

ATK/1650 DEF/1700

MRD-039 Bottom Dweller

DESTROYER GOLEM

[ROCK]
A golem with a massive right hand for crushing its victims.

ATK/1500 DEF/1000

MRD-040 Destroyer Golem

KAMINARI ATTACK

[THUNDER / FUSION]
"Ocubeam" + "Mega Thunderball"

ATK/1900 DEF/1400

MRD-041 Kaminari Attack

RAINBOW FLOWER

[PLANT / EFFECT]
This monster may attack your opponent's Life Points directly.

ATK/ 400 DEF/ 500

MRD-042 Rainbow Flower

MORINPHEN

[FIEND]
A strange fiend with long arms and razor-sharp talons.

ATK/1550 DEF/1300

MRD-043 Morinphen

MEGA THUNDERBALL

[THUNDER]
Rolls along the ground releasing bolts of electricity to attack its enemies.

ATK/ 750 DEF/ 600

MRD-044 Mega Thunderball

TONGYO

[FISH]
This monster captures other fish with its long tongue and sucks the energy out of them.

ATK/1350 DEF/ 800

MRD-045 Tongyo

EMPRESS JUDGE

[WARRIOR / FUSION]
"Queen's Double" + "Takuhme"

ATK/2100 DEF/1700

MRD-046 Empress Judge

PALE BEAST 地

[BEAST]
With skin tinged a bluish-white, this strange creature is a fearsome sight to behold.

ATK/1500 DEF/1200

MRD-047 Pale Beast

ELECTRIC LIZARD 地

[THUNDER / EFFECT]
A non-Zombie-Type monster attacking "Electric Lizard" cannot attack on its following turn.

ATK/850 DEF/800

MRD-048 Electric Lizard

HUNTER SPIDER 地

[INSECT]
This monster feeds on whatever it catches in its web.

ATK/1600 DEF/1400

MRD-049 Hunter Spider

ANCIENT LIZARD WARRIOR 地

[REPTILE]
Before the dawn of man, this lizard warrior ruled supreme.

ATK/1400 DEF/1100

MRD-050 Ancient Lizard Warrior

QUEEN'S DOUBLE 地

[WARRIOR / EFFECT]
This monster may attack your opponent's Life Points directly.

ATK/350 DEF/300

MRD-051 Queen's Double

TRENT 地

[PLANT]
A guardian of the woods, this massive tree is believed to be immortal.

ATK/1500 DEF/1800

MRD-052 Trent

DISK MAGICIAN 闇

[MACHINE]
This monster hides in a saucer and only appears when executing an attack.

ATK/1350 DEF/1000

MRD-053 Disk Magician

HYOSUBE 水

[AQUA]
This amphibian is strong on the attack, but leaves much to be desired when defending.

ATK/1500 DEF/900

MRD-054 Hyosube

HIBIKIME 地

[WARRIOR]
Confuses enemy monsters with a noise that is harsh to the ears.

ATK/1450 DEF/1000

MRD-055 Hibikime

SOUL RELEASE 魔

[MAGIC CARD]

Select up to 5 cards from either you or your opponent's Graveyard and remove them from the current Duel.

MRD-058 Soul Release

THE CHEERFUL COFFIN 魔

[MAGIC CARD]

You can discard up to 3 Monster Cards from your hand to the Graveyard.

MRD-059 The Cheerful Coffin

BABY DRAGON 風

[DRAGON]
Much more than just a child, this dragon is gifted with untapped power.

ATK/1200 DEF/700

MRD-061 Baby Dragonm

BLACKLAND FIRE DRAGON 闇

[DRAGON]
A dragon that dwells in the depths of darkness, its vulnerability lies in its poor eyesight.

ATK/1500 DEF/800

MRD-062 Blackland Fire Dragon

SWAMP BATTLEGUARD 地

[WARRIOR / EFFECT]
Increase the ATK of this monster by 500 points for every face-up "Lava Battleguard" on your side of the field.

ATK/1800 DEF/1500

MRD-063 Swamp Battleguard

BATTLE STEER 地

[BEAST-WARRIOR]
A bull monster often found in the woods, it charges enemy monsters with a pair of deadly horns.

ATK/1800 DEF/1300

MRD-064 Battle Steer

SAGGI THE DARK CLOWN 闇

[SPELLCASTER]
This clown appears from nowhere and executes very strange moves to avoid enemy attacks.

ATK/600 DEF/1500

MRD-066 Saggi the Dark Clown

MRD-067 Dragon Piper

MRD-068 Illusionist Faceless Mage

MRD-070 Great Moth

MRD-072 Jellyfish

MRD-073 Castle of Dark Illusions

MRD-074 King of Yamimakai

MRD-056 Fake Trap

MRD-076 Mystic Horseman

MRD-077 Rabid Horseman

MRD-078 Crass Clown

MRD-079 Pumpking the King of Ghosts

MRD-080 Dream Clown

MRD-081 Tainted Wisdom

MRD-082 Ancient Brain

MRD-083 Guardian of the Labyrinth

MRD-084 Prevent Rat

MRD-085 The Little Swordsman of Aile

MRD-086 Princess of Tsurugi

MRD-087 Protector of the Throne

MRD-088 Tremendous Fire

MRD-089 Jirai Gumo

MRD-091 Labyrinth Tank

MRD-092 Ryu-Kishin Powered

MRD-093 Bickuribox

MRD-094 Giltia the D. Knight

MRD-095 Launcher Spider

MRD-096 Giga-Tech Wolf

MRD-097 Thunder Dragon

MRD-098 7 Colored Fish

MRD-099 The Immortal of Thunder

MRD-100 Punished Eagle

MRD-101 Insect Soldiers of the Sky

HOSHININGEN

[FAIRY/EFFECT]
As long as this card remains face-up on the field, increase the ATK of all LIGHT monsters by 500 points and decrease the ATK of all DARK monsters by 400 points.

ATK/ 500 DEF/ 700

MRD-102 Hoshiningen

MUSICIAN KING

[SPELLCASTER/FUSION]
"Witch of the Black Forest" + "Lady of Faith"

ATK/1750 DEF/1500

MRD-103 Musician King

YADO KARU

[AQUA/EFFECT]
When this card is changed from Defense Position to Attack Position, you can place any number of cards from your hand at the bottom of your Deck in any order you desire.

ATK/ 900 DEF/1700

MRD-104 Yado Karu

CYBER SAURUS

[MACHINE/FUSION]
"Blast Juggler" + "Two-Headed King Rex"

ATK/1800 DEF/1400

MRD-105 Cyber Saurus

CANNON SOLDIER

[MACHINE/EFFECT]
Offer 1 monster on your side of the field as a Tribute to inflict 500 points of Direct Damage to your opponent's Life Points. Monsters used for a Tribute Summon or that are offered as Tributes due to other cards' effects are excluded.

ATK/1400 DEF/1300

MRD-106 Cannon Soldier

THE BISTRO BUTCHER

[FIEND/EFFECT]
When this card inflicts damage to your opponent, your opponent must draw 2 cards from his/her Deck.

ATK/1800 DEF/1000

MRD-108 The Bistro Butcher

STAR BOY

[AQUA/EFFECT]
As long as this card remains face-up on the field, increase the ATK of all WATER monsters by 500 points and decrease the ATK of all FIRE monsters by 400 points.

ATK/ 550 DEF/ 500

MRD-109 Star Boy

MILUS RADIANT

[BEAST/EFFECT]
As long as this card remains face-up on the field, increase the ATK of all EARTH monsters by 500 points and decrease the ATK of all WIND monsters by 400 points.

ATK/ 300 DEF/ 250

MRD-110 Milus Radiant

FLAME CEREBRUS

[PYRO]
Known to roam as the "Burning Executioner", this monster is capable of burning enemies to cinders.

ATK/2100 DEF/1800

MRD-111 Flame Cerebrus

NIWATORI

[WINGED BEAST]
Swallows enemies whole and uses their essence as energy.

ATK/ 900 DEF/ 800

MRD-112 Niwatori

DARK ELF

[SPELLCASTER/EFFECT]
This card requires a cost of 1000 of your own Life Points to attack.

ATK/2000 DEF/ 800

MRD-113 Dark Elf

MUSHROOM MAN #2

[WARRIOR/EFFECT]
A player controlling this monster loses 500 Life Points during each of his/her Standby Phases when this card is face-up on the field. Control of this card is shifted to your opponent by paying 500 Life Points at your own End Phase.

ATK/1250 DEF/ 800

MRD-114 Mushroom Man #2

LAVA BATTLEGUARD

[WARRIOR/EFFECT]
Increase the ATK of this card by 500 points for each face-up "Swamp Battleguard" on your side of the field.

ATK/1550 DEF/1800

MRD-115 Lava Battleguard

WITCH OF THE BLACK FOREST

[SPELLCASTER/EFFECT]
When this card is sent from the field to the Graveyard, select 1 monster with a DEF of 1500 or less from your Deck to your hand. Your Deck is then shuffled.

ATK/1100 DEF/1200

MRD-116 Witch of the Black Forest

LITTLE CHIMERA

[BEAST/EFFECT]
As long as this card remains face-up on the field, increase the ATK of all FIRE monsters by 500 points and decrease the ATK of all WATER monsters by 400 points.

ATK/ 600 DEF/ 550

MRD-117 Little Chimera

BLADEFLY

[INSECT/EFFECT]
As long as this card remains face-up on the field, increase the ATK of all WIND monsters by 500 points and decrease the ATK of all EARTH monsters by 400 points.

ATK/ 600 DEF/ 700

MRD-118 Bladefly

MRD-119 Lady of Faith

MRD-120 Twin-Headed T. Dragon

MRD-121 Witch's Apprentice

MRD-122 Blue-Winged Crown

MRD-123 Skull Knight

MRD-124 Gazelle the King of Myth. Beasts

MRD-125 Garnecia Elefantis

MRD-131 Shield & Sword

MRD-132 Sword of Deep-Seated

MRD-133 Block Attack

MRD-134 The Unhappy Maiden

MRD-135 Robbin' Goblin

MRD-136 Germ Infection

MRD-137 Paralyzing Potion

MRD-139 Ring of Magnetism

MRD-140 Share the Pain